To  your photo
The ... ng us toget
on ... g magasine.
In ...

lots of loves

from

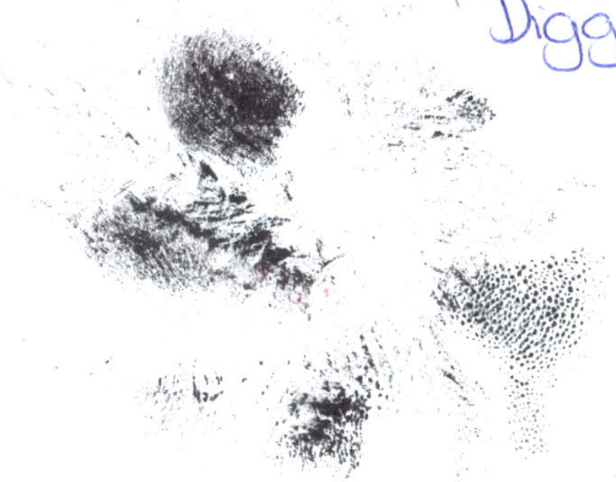

Digger

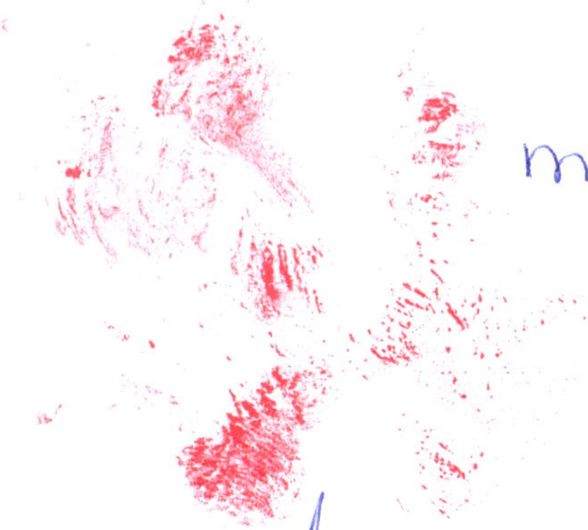

mollie

& Julie

First Published in May 2017 by Julie Campbell

Text and photographs copyright of Julie Campbell

Find us on face book; WWW.facebook.com/500miles2015

Tails of Two Sprollies

(Walking for Wildlife and Woofers)
By
Mollie and Digger Campbell

Have you ever had something happen to you, just a small seemingly insignificant occurrence, that for some reason sends your life hurtling down a totally different path?

Well that is what happened to us…. and it all began with a tiny hedgehog!

This book tells you about the first two crazy years of our "Furry Fundraising" as we walked hundreds of miles to raise money for wildlife and dog rescues. We hope that you enjoy it.

Lots of "Woofs" from Mollie and Digger

Who are we?

Let us introduce ourselves. We are Mollie and Digger.

We are Sprollies (Springer Spaniel / Border Collie crossed.)
Yes! That does make us a bit crazy! We have very good chasing skills and lots of bounce!

We are brother and sister and we were born to our dad Harris the Springer and our mum Patch the Border Collie.

We live with Harris on a Farm in Yorkshire, England. Sadly our mum Patch passed away in 2016.

We look after two humans. The male one is called Murdo. He is Scottish, a bit crazy and he is a farmer. The female one is called Julie and she sells car parts. Julie is a bit daft and the is the one that comes with us on our fund-raising walks. Julie is from Lancashire but has been living in Yorkshire for 17 years.

Mollie

Mollie (AKA Mollie-the-sprollie, Moll-Sproll, & Sprollie Monster) is our humans' first Sprollie. She was born on their farm in July 2009.

She is a bit of a tearaway at times and a bit spaced out at others. Mollie is loving and gentle when indoors, loves her cuddles and being groomed. She is known to pretend to be wet so that she can be towel dried and if she wants the humans to stroke her, she strokes them!

Outdoors Mollie is like a steam train on full power. There is no stopping her. She can run for miles and will not come back.

Mollie loves wallowing in mud (she must have been a hippo in a past life) she also loves children and rabbits. She hates guns and fireworks.

Digger

Digger (AKA Dig-Dog, Diggy Wiggles and Diggy-Boo) was born in 2012 and is Mollie's younger brother.

He was originally named Buster and was due to go and live on the Isle Of Skye with male human's brother Peter. Julie fell in love with him in the meantime and pleaded to let him stay with us instead.

Digger loves digging which explains why he was renamed. He likes lying on top of his humans and having his ears stroked, going for walks, biscuits, biscuits and more biscuits.

Digger has a "Biscuit Dance" which he performs by the treat cupboard. It is a mash up of all the tricks he learned as a pup. It goes something like "Right paw, left paw, down, sit, repeat." He knows that it will always guarantee him a biscuit.

Digger is a coward and is scared of pretty much everything else. Particularly the ironing board!

Julie

Julie has always been a dog lover from being a baby. Her parents taught her to love the outdoors and nature. She was camping and "walking" in the Yorkshire Dales before she was even walking (on her dad's back) and carried on as a child and teenager walking for miles and miles just to see what was "Out There."

Julie loves her Doggies, walking, animals, photography, the great outdoors, gardening, cooking and crafts. She dislikes cruelty, negativity and celery!

How it all began...

During the summer of 2014, human Julie decided to get fit. Due to her love of the Great Outdoors she decided to begin jogging and promptly installed a GPS tracking and measuring App on her phone. She managed a three mile jog on just four occasions. The fourth being the time she wrecked her ankle. She was in pain, swollen and hobbling for seven weeks. The doctor decided that pounding along the streets didn't agree with her ankles. She was told to give it up or do something less strenuous like walking. Slightly hooked on the app, Julie wanted to carry on using it and get out and about. She decided instead to increase the length of our weekend walks. This was fantastic news for us. Long distance walks were something we could all get involved in.

Due to Julie's long working hours, we were only guaranteed Sunday as a walking day with her. The rest of the week our male human walked us. We were only logging our walks with Julie as it was her fitness challenge so we had to make the most of her Sundays off, the occasional Saturdays and her holiday time.

In 2014 we managed to walk 385 miles on our days with Julie. We decided that in 2015 we would set a challenge to walk 500 miles.

In late 2014, while we had this 500 mile challenge in

mind, we set off on a local walk and spotted a little prickly ball in a cattle-grid. As dogs that prefer cuddles to ball games we wouldn't normally have paid any attention to it but this ball seemed to be snuffling around down there. The humans fished it out and saw that it was a hedgehog. The hedgehog was very small. It should have still been with its mum and it was much too small to make it through hibernation.

Julie phoned The British Hedgehog Preservation Society who gave her the number of a local lady called Marianne. Marianne ran a local wildlife rescue and told Julie to bring the hedgehog over immediately. On arrival at the wildlife sanctuary, the hedgehog was given fluids and medication and a nice warm place to sleep. Marianne would keep it and feed it up over winter and release it in the spring. Julie had wanted to give the sanctuary a donation to help with the care of the hedgehog but in her rush to get the hedgehog to safety, she had forgotten her purse. She took the details of their Facebook page instead and promised to send a donation. On checking out the page, we realised that the sanctuary was struggling to stay open due to funding. We wondered how we could help.

When a friend asked us if we were walking the 500 miles for charity we knew just what to do! On the 1st of January 2015 we began our "Walk for Wildlife" in aid of Marianne's Sanctuary.

500 miles in 2015

Our first walk of 2015 began on the first day of the year. Prior to our challenge, our walks were usually 3 miles long. We were keen to extend the distance and on this day we walked just over 6 miles, passing over a section of the Pennine Way and up onto Elslack Moor to a trig pillar called Pinhaw Beacon. It was a very windy day and Julie tried to make a short video about our walk but it was too windy to hear what she was saying.

On following walks she wasn't overly entertaining when she wrote the blog. It was all "Blah blah blah.... We walked five miles..... My legs hurt....." so we sprollies decided to get to grips with the computer and take over. We told tales of our walks and life with our human. The hassles of owning a human. The things we do to entertain her. There was plenty to write about. After finishing each of our walks, Julie set about organising the photos and we went on-line and told everyone what a fool she had made of herself that day. Julie is hugely talented in the "fling yourself on the ground" department and at things like getting lost and getting poop on her fingers due to flyaway bags when she is scooping. It is always good to watch, just for a laugh.

By March we had reached a quarter of our 500 mile

target and the donations were coming in. Our Facebook blog was attracting more followers and we were having a great time.

April brought our human more embarrassment when she tried to rescue a randy frog. We were having fun running in and out of a river and Julie spotted the frog on the path. It was in danger of being trampled by us, as we hadn't seen it. As our paws landed dangerously close to it, Julie scooped it up and the frog clung to her fingers. It had such a vice like grip that Julie couldn't free it and she filmed it on her phone and posted it to our blog. Us doggies (and most of our followers) howled with laughter as the comments from the wildlife lovers came in and we were told that the frog was trying to mate with Julie's hand.

May brought us sunshine and lots of canal walks and both of us dogs fell in on different occasions and it was Julie's turn to laugh at us. We were loving our new adventures and the miles and the money were racking up. Our walks took us all over, up hills and down valleys, along rivers and through fields. In sunshine, rain, wind and fog.

By June we had reached 300 miles and raised £800 but we received some sad news. The rescue that we were supporting had shut down. Stuck mid-challenge without a cause, we wondered what to do next. Then by pure chance Emma at Little Silver Hedgehog began to follow our blog. We asked her if we could support her rescue. Emma was thrilled to have us dogs walking for her hedgehogs. Emma worked within a support group of other five other rescues and she asked us to share any money raised with them. With now six rescues to support rather than just the one, we had to find other ways of increasing the money we raised. We began to sell bagged sweets to friends and colleagues.

Our walking continued throughout the year and in September, with the help of male human, his brother Peter and Peter's family, we reached our 500th mile. It was the best walk ever. On a beautiful day on the Isle of Skye, we walked over the moors, passing Dunvegan Castle and through stunning scenery along the coast. We ended the walk on a coral beach, paddling in the sea while the humans drank Prosecco as the sun set.

We continued to walk and raise funds until we hit 600 miles on the 31st December. We raised £2239 in total. People were asking us to carry on in 2016. They were also asking us to raise money for dogs because most of our fans were dog lovers. We found a local charity called Pendle Dogs In Need and added it to our group of rescues. We changed our title from "Walk for Wildlife" to "Walk for Wildlife and Woofers" and on the 1st of January 2016 we began a new challenge of walking "6 Ways in 2016." This would consist of us walking 6 "Ways" (long distance walks) and attempting to beat our previous year's mileage.

The rest of our book will concentrate on our "6 Ways in 2016" challenge, but first let us tell you a little bit about each of our rescues.

Little Silver Hedgehog

A hedgehog hospital in York, run by Emma Farley, caring for poorly and injured wild hedgehogs for over 5 years.

Emma creates handmade silver jewellery inspired by nature and wildlife. The proceeds help to buy food, medicines and equipment. Emma's rescue work is entirely self-funded. She began rescuing after finding a hedgehog that had become trapped in the mesh from a fat ball. Emma then found Dr Toni Bunnell who taught her the basics of hedgehog rescue.

Visit Emma's page for details of her Jewellery and the hedgehogs that she has rescued.

www.facebook.com/littlesilverhedgehog

www.littlesilverhedgehog.wordpress.com

Pendle Dogs in Need

Nurse Paula Knowles and primary school Headteacher Sharon Ashley launched Pendle Dogs in Need in April 2013 to re-home unwanted dogs from around Pendle which get dumped on the streets. They use experienced foster homes to assess dogs that come in from the pound, then they profile them on their Facebook page in the hope that a forever home will be found. All potential homes are checked before adoption. They rely totally on donations.
www.facebook.com/PendleDogsInNeed
www.pendledogsinneed.co.uk

Whitby Wildlife Sanctuary

Run by Alexandra Farmer, the sanctuary operates 24/7, 365 days a year to rescue and care for all sick, injured and orphaned wildlife from Yorkshire and Country Durham. They care for over 1200 animals every year.
Alex has recently become a registered charity and she often takes in animals from the smaller rescues. The sanctuary relies on donations and fundraising.
www.facebook.com/whitbywildlifesanctuary.
www.whitbywildlife.co.uk

Hope for Hedgehogs

Run by Amber Glossop in Ascot, Berkshire. Amber has always been passionate about hedgehogs but as more and more started visiting her garden her interest in them grew. She wanted to get more involved in their care and welfare so Amber booked herself onto a course via the BHPS at Vale Wildlife Hospital. Amber funds all their food and medication herself (as do the majority of carers.) and she has a wonderful vet who steps in to help. Her vet says "If we can work together and save a little hedgehog we must be doing something good"
Visit Amber and her hedgehogs at;
www.facebook.com/Hopeforhedgehogs

H.A.P.P.Y - Hedgehog Appreciation Prickly Pals Yorkshire

A hedgehog rescue set up in October 2014 by Jacqui and Pete Morrell. They rely on donations and their wages to support the hogs. Jacqui and Pete have an indoor "Hogspital" and outdoor hutches for all the rescue hogs. They are fortunate to have great local support from Dr Toni Bunnell from York. H.A.P.P.Y's aim is to raise awareness of the dangers to hedgehogs including extinction and to positively promote these beautiful creatures.
www.facebook.com/HAPPY-hedgehog-appreciation-prickly-pals-Yorkshire-754889337902021

Help York's Hedgehogs

Dr Toni Bunnell is a musician, a singer-songwriter, an author and a wildlife biologist. She has run her hedgehog rescue centre since 1990 working in conjunction with York RSPCA. She is actively engaged in research in hedgehog ecology and conservation and is conducting a long-term project involving monitoring hedgehogs within York.

Toni has appeared on Love your Garden, Countryfile and other prime-time television and radio programmes such as Radio 4, 'The World Tonight'.

www.facebook.com/Help-Yorks-Hedgehogs-132231550201521

Sleepy Hollow Hedgehog Rescue

Run by Claire Robinson since 2014 in Scarborough. Claire always loved hedgehogs since she was young and she has fed wild hedgehogs in her garden for many years. As she learned more about them she started weighing the ones in the garden in autumn to see if they were heavy enough for hibernation. Claire signed up on two courses before setting up a rescue. Claire says "It is hard to juggle with work but I wouldn't change it for the world" Visit her at

www.facebook.com/Sleepy-Hollow-Hedgehog-Rescue-1576880179236909

Julie Hallucinates!

When you have been walking for wildlife and woofers for two years, it begins to take over your mind.

While us doggies are always searching for wildlife on our walks, Julie is constantly imagining things.

We have had home grown carrots that looked like legs and a hedgehog and she has tried to rescue a hedgehog that turned out to be a lump of moss.

Julie has found faces in stones and also a stone that looked like a hedgehog ornament that she owns.

The daft human has even stopped the van in the middle of the road in order to rescue an injured blackbird.... and it turned out to be a bag of dog poop.

6 Ways in 2016

In 2016 we decided to walk 6 Ways (long distance walks) We chose a mixture, from the short Pennine Bridleway Settle Loop and the longer 25 mile Yorkshire Three Peaks. The 45 mile circular Pendle Way and the 50 mile Calderdale Way. The most difficult logistically were the 84 mile Dales Way and 100 mile Lady Anne's Way which both stretched right up the country.

The Calderdale Way

The Calderdale Way is a circular walk passing through Brighouse, Ripponden, Todmorden, Hebden Bridge and Queensbury among other smaller towns.

The Calderdale Way as a long distance walk was our first and our worst! Now don't get us wrong, we did enjoy it. It was great fun and a wonderful adventure but the time of year crossed with the fact that we overdid it with the mileage, made it a bit of a killer compared to the rest.

When we announced in January 2016 that we were taking on this walk, Julie's brother-in-law Lee told us that he too was planning on completing it. It made sense to do it together. Lee was put in charge of the planning and mapping and Julie was in charge of driving and food. Lee is an experienced long distance walker so we felt that we would be in safe hands with him. Unfortunately he did make one mistake... He let Julie choose the duration of the walk. Now, looking at other people's blogs and information on the internet, most people tend to do it over four or sometimes five days. Julie being keen to get going, a bit over excited and not wanting to waste too many days off work, decided to do it in three consecutive days. Julie is a fool!

We decided to begin the walk on the 18th February. It had been quite wet for weeks and weeks before then and it was also pretty cold. Julie hadn't read up too much about the walk other than things of interest to look out for. She doesn't like to find out too much beforehand because she likes to just see things for herself without any prior expectations. Once having done a walk, she will then read into it a bit more afterwards. She is odd like that! So in typical Julie style, she just conducted a brief internet search the week before and then panicked!

Julie read that "The Calderdale Way is a challenging 50 mile walk exploring hills, moors and valleys. It is a very "up and down" journey with few level sections. The walk has a total climb of 22 metres per mile making it an equivalent distance to a flat 57.49 miles." This did not sound good. Even with us turbo powered dogs to help, Julie is terrible at climbing hills and not much better at descending them. We were slightly worried that we may not manage it. This is how we got on...

Day 1, by Mollie

I was woken at 5 am by a very excited but very tired Julie. She had not slept for two nights. She packed a rucksack containing lots of things, dressed herself in her winter walking gear and put me on my lead. We ventured outside into the frost and I sat on the passenger seat of the van, watching patiently while Julie scraped the ice off the windscreen. It was

FREEZING! We set off on a very slippery journey to go and collect Lee, before driving to Brighouse, the start of our walk, and parking the van at the train station. The plan was to walk to Todmorden and then catch the train back. On the way there the radio played "Walk this Way" by the rock band Aerosmith which we (or maybe just Julie) screeched along to as she drove. She thought it was very apt for the walk. I thought it was just noise! Terrible noise!

At Brighouse we walked down the road towards the canal which is where we met the Calderdale Way. At 6.50am we joined the tow-path behind two men who were smoking something rather smelly. The humans were a bit shocked and I felt a bit giddy though goodness knows why.

Further along the canal I decided to start early and demonstrate to Lee one of my favourite tricks. It was the "Pull out the extendable lead as far as you can and wrap it round every leg" trick. You know the one? It's where you get in the biggest tangle ever and then when the humans try and unravel you, you sit down so that your legs are hidden beneath you and they can't get at you. Lee was perplexed. Julie was annoyed. I was ecstatic. It worked like a dream.

As we left the canal we spotted our first C.W logo, painted on the stone wall by the side of the path. We were going the right way which makes a change for Julie. We crossed a road and encountered the first of many hills, leading up into some woods. This was where Julie thought she saw a big dog in the trees and made us all stand quietly and look. It turned out to be one of three deer. They were up on the brow of the hill. The humans tried to photograph them but I was so excited to see them that I screamed and screamed like I was being murdered (don't ask, it's just something I do) and I scared the deer away.

We exited the wood and followed some old steps called "Cat Steps" down a hill. I don't know why they are called this. I didn't see any cats! The stones along the walls at either side of the steps had really old carvings on them and the humans found it very interesting. I was just keen to get going and into the next lot of trees called Cromwell Wood. It was a very cold day but dry and sunny. The ground was very boggy in places due to the recent rains and slippery in others due to the icy temperatures. We had some very steep hills to climb which gave us some amazing views over the towns below but also made Julie struggle. The surrounding towns in this area are mainly old mill towns and have a dark industrial feel about them. In summer they may seem a bit more inviting but at this time of year they seemed rather gloomy.

The walk took us onto a road, through fields and into more woods.... eventually.... as we got a bit confused and carried on up the road instead of turning into them. These woods had steps leading through and up the hillside and a bridge covered in ice. It was so funny to watch the humans struggling to cross it. The steps were very steep and when we reached a stile in the wall at the top, Julie's legs were so tired that she got wedged on the wall. She was unable to move to get back down the other side.

The walk then took us over Norland Moor, which was lovely and flat and wonderfully boggy. Around a third of the way across it there was a trig pillar, next to which was a bench. We decided to stop for lunch and dog treats. It was so cold up there, even with my furry coat. We didn't stay for long. We needed to keep moving to stay warm.

A lot of the walk is through grass and woods, so when we reached Ripponden we stopped for a few minutes to admire the old cottages, cobbled streets and church. As we crossed the road, Lee spotted a hair salon on the other side called "Mollie's Salon" next door to which was a dog grooming salon with giant paws on the window. Julie went and took photos of it as she thought it was funny that I should appear to own a salon.

On leaving Ripponden we had to climb yet another hill. Despite the cold weather, Julie was working up a sweat and decided to remove her hat and scarf. She obviously jinxed us because within five minutes it was snowing!

We were quite a way into the walk by now and it

was becoming apparent that we would be walking a lot more than the 20 miles we had estimated. We weren't doing it in great time either as paths were either really boggy or littered with uneven rocks. We needed to get a move on. I dragged Julie as hard as I could up the hillside but she was tiring and struggled.

We continued uphill to Withens Clough Reservoir and by the time we reached it we were caught in a blizzard. I had snow clinging to my fur and the humans had hail and snow in their eyes. None of us could see where we were going. The wind drove the snow into the humans's hoods and it began to run down their backs. Julie's gloves were heavily soaked, but to take them off made her hands freeze in the bitter wind. I was very tough and carried on for the sake of the animals that we were helping.

We had a bit of respite over the moors as the terrain flattened out. The snow petered out and the sun was beginning to set. It looked pretty spectacular above the snow covered moorland. However the sun setting at this point was not great. We still had quite a way to walk. My paws were cold and sore.

As The Calderdale Way crossed The Pennine Way, we saw Stoodley Pike Monument on our right. An old packhorse route took us downhill towards Mankinholes. This was the worst part of the walk for us. We were frozen and exhausted. I had given up and just wanted to sit down and sleep. Julie's legs were tired and stiffening up in the cold. She had started to shiver so much that she has lost control of her jaw and it was jigging about all over the place. The route was made up of old stone slabs that were worn down quite low in the centre. They were very difficult to walk on but then so was the boggy ground at the side of them. It was slippery on both and the descent was quite dicey. Julie and I kept stopping and Lee was worried as Julie was shivering so much. He urged us to keep going or we'd catch hypothermia. We carried on. We had to. Julie was trying not to cry. I was whimpering.

What felt like an eternity later we finally reached Todmorden and the warmth of the waiting room in the train station. However things didn't improve much there. The train was a 40 minute wait away and the room was quite tiny, so when a gang of 12 teenage boys came in and began to cause trouble, we were trapped and quite scared. Julie had wrapped me in a towel as I couldn't stop shaking. Nor could I stay awake. When my head fell on the feet of one of the boys he started swearing. We put up with it for a while just to stay in the warm room, however they were out of control and we had to vacate to the cold platform. When the Transport Police arrived to sort the gang out, they all ended up on the platform too, shouting and arguing with the officers. Luckily when the train arrived, they didn't get on and we were safe and warm once more.

We finally arrived home at 9pm, 15.5 hours after we had set off. We had walked 26.6 miles in total due to the parts where we had gone off track and the bits in between the route and our transport. The first day of The Calderdale Way had been a good but challenging experience and far more difficult than we had ever imagined. Julie was exhausted and had huge blisters on her feet. The thought of doing it all the next day made her get a bit teary. When Murdo told her to cancel it as it was too much for her, she replied "No! I said I would do it so I will!" Julie didn't sleep that night either due to the pain and the thought of continuing tomorrow. I slept like I always do. Like a dog!

Day 2, By Digger

I was told that the second part of the Calderdale Way would be mine to walk. However when the morning arrived and I saw Julie doing a strange kind of hobble into the kitchen and that Mollie couldn't even stand up, I panicked. I tried to hide away in order to get out of going but Julie found me behind the settee.

Our humans checked Mollie out and she appeared to be broken. Julie said that she felt like a very bad mummy! I wasn't overly keen on going through the same thing and promptly scuttled off to bed to hide again.

Once Julie had told me that today's walk was shorter and reminded me that it was for charity, I felt a bit better. We picked Lee up and drove to a small village called Pecket Well. We parked the van and walked for two miles into Hebden Bridge where we then caught a big scary train to a town called Todmorden.

Now I am not well travelled on trains and I am pretty much scared of everything, so on sitting down, I decided to hide under the seat in front. I crawled so far under that I popped out between another passenger's legs.

On our arrival at Todmorden we crossed the road, the canal and then the railway bridge before ascending a very steep hill. We were right up above the town and had a great ariel view, however the steep cliff-like drop to our left made us all feel a bit nervous. As we passed through the fields along the next stretch, we could see Stoodley Pike far away on the hillside to our right. The humans could not believe that it looked so far away considering that it was towards the end of yesterday's walk. The humans were chattering away about their shared ambition of writing a book. As we write this a year later, Lee has a book published and us Sprollies are writing this one and Julie, well she is still dreaming...

The route took us back downhill, between a school and park to the road that we crossed earlier on. We were just a little bit further along. We crossed over and walked past the houses until the route took us off to the right, under a railway bridge and up a huge, snaking, steep hill. "This walk is ALL uphill!" wailed Julie, as she struggled her way to the top.

Eventually the path evened out a bit as we walked along Whirlaw Common. We passed by a farmhouse and some Collie dogs came to greet us from the window of the hayloft. I woofed to say "Hello" and they woofed back. Further along we reached a farm where they had Deer and some strange things called Emus. I had never seen anything as odd in my life! I was a bit of a wuss because I was missing my sister Mollie. I don't like going for walks without her and I cried a little bit. We stopped for lunch and dog treats on a bench at the top of Todmorden Golf Course before continuing towards Heptonstall.

The humans really liked it at Heptonstall. It was very old and there was a ruined church which we looked around and lots of the houses had stone carvings above the doors. I sniffed all the smells as we passed through.

At Midgehole we didn't see any midges or holes, just a path up through more steep woodland towards Pecket Well. Again, the path was almost on the edge of a cliff and the last part of the walk was quite scary due to the slippery path and the steep drop.

We walked 15 miles in total which was more than enough for me. I'm not as keen as Mollie on the longer walks. Julie was exhausted yet again but glad that there was only one more day to go.

Day 3

When Julie woke us in the morning, she was hoping that maybe both of us dogs could do the final walk, despite us being a nightmare when we are together.

Unfortunately, we were so sore and tired that neither of us could even stand up. We felt terrible at letting everyone down but the previous two days had been too much for our little paws. We sent Julie off on her own. She didn't mind, she thought we had done enough miles between us and it meant that the last stretch would be a bit easier for her as we do tend to drag her around like a rag doll.

By the sound of it we didn't miss much. The humans left the van at Brighouse Station once more, ready for the journey home at the end of the route. A train took them to Hebden Bridge where they decided to get a taxi rather than walk up the steep hill to yesterday's finish point, Pecket Well.

By the time they reached their starting point for the day it had begun to rain. It didn't stop all day. A track led them up behind a farm and onto the extremely boggy Wadsworth Moor. The path skirted along the edge of the moor and they trudged along it, heads down to avoid the wind and rain. They didn't talk much as they couldn't hear each other for the wind. When they ended up at a reservoir and a ruined barn, they realised they had walked too far and missed a turning. It was frustrating having to track their way back. Down in Luddenden Dean, things were a little more interesting as they passed through a campsite and nature reserve and the route took the humans across the river and up through the woods.

Lunch break was held at Queensbury on a main

road in a bus shelter. There were no seats but at least lunch was eaten out of the rain. The road from here was a bit grotty and took the humans up Crooked Lane which had become a local fly tipping area. Julie was keen to get off that road but the next part was disturbing in another way...

Crossing the road they followed a path that ran down a hill between a wall along the roadside on the left and another wall along the edge of some woodland on the right. This area was called Shibden Dale. The path veered right just as the wall by the wood ended. As the humans took the right turn, a man walked out from behind the wall. It was as though he had been waiting for them. He was quite a stocky man, dressed in green and camouflage as if he was a hunter. He asked what the humans were doing in the wood. He told of people coming down there to shoot deer and then leaving them bleeding and dying in the trees. He made Julie and Lee feel a little bit uncomfortable, it seemed as though he may have been the hunter and that they had disturbed him. They explained that they were walking the Calderdale Way but as they walked down the muddy and steep path, he followed them. He said that the hill was called "Hanging Hill" and that in the olden days, criminals were given a chance to escape their fate by running away up the hill. The ones that made it to the top were allowed to escape. The ones that didn't make it were hung in the trees. Julie told us that it was a bit like being in a horror movie and that she had visions of getting to the bottom and the man producing a gun and telling them to run back up the hill or be killed. If he had done that, Julie would have been a goner. Three days on the Calderdale Way had left her with no energy whatsoever.

As the humans and their stalker reached the bottom of the hill, the man pointed out a huge abandoned house called Scout Hall. He said that the locals called it "The house of a thousand windows." He urged them to go and have a closer look at the carved hunting scene above the door, but Julie said that it was very eerie down there and they were losing time. Later, at home, Julie researched the house and found that it was a hunting lodge built in 1681 for a local silk merchant. It is what is called a Calender House as it was made up of 12 bays, 52 doors and 365 panes of glass. It is grade 2 listed but now it stands in ruins. Just an empty windowless shell.

The third section was, once more, longer than expected and like the first section, darkness fell while the humans were still walking. As they neared the end, they could not see a thing. It made the navigation almost impossible. They were both desperate to reach the end, yet the twinkling lights of Brighouse seemed very far away in the distance. They had to cross through a field and their torches weren't overly great. They didn't want to use both at once in case the batteries didn't last to the end of the walk. The field was so boggy that they began to sink and they had no idea where the path was other than to the right. Suddenly they heard a noise. There

was a horse in there with them and it had been spooked by the light. Neither human has much experience with horses and are a bit wary of them. Especially when the horse is making a racket and they are in total darkness and sinking into the mud. They tried to get out of the field fast, using Julies mapping app on her phone to guide them to the gate. Something was a bit amiss though because where the gate was shown on the map, there was nothing but a fence cordoning off a huge drop. They ran towards some stables and jumped over the gate to safety. Standing in the stable yard they felt like they were trespassing and they could see no other way out than through someone's garden and up a driveway. They were so relieved to make it to the road without getting caught trespassing.

After that, a decision was made to avoid the remaining fields (also containing horses) and stick to the road for safety. They arrived back at Brighouse after completing 22 miles, exhausted yet over the moon that they had finished the walk. It had been a very difficult walk but also very rewarding. Though after that, the decision was made to make our future walks a little more enjoyable and less punishing by splitting them up in a sensible manner. As much as we wanted to challenge ourselves and raise money, we wanted to stay safe and healthy in the process.

The Pendle Way

The Pendle Way is as the name suggests, a "Way" (or long distance walk) around the area of Pendle in Lancashire. It is a 45 mile circular route and begins at the Pendle Heritage Centre at Barrowford. It takes in towns such as Barnoldswick, Thornton-in-Craven, Wycoller, Reedley, Newchurch and includes a climb up Pendle Hill. Due to the area being associated with the legends of the Pendle Witches, the sign posts for the walk show a witch riding a broomstick. It was the most local of all our 6 Ways so quite easy for us transport-wise and it was a well marked steady route.

Day 1 by Mollie

We began the walk in March on Julie's birthday and the sun was shining brightly. Julie said that it was "The best birthday walk ever!" We got a lift to the start point in Barrowford and met Julie's mum Lynn and two of her dogs, our brothers, Toby and Jack. We followed a narrow path along a river and crossed the road heading out to a place where two rivers meet. It was called Water-Meetings, near Blacko. On our way there we bumped into Julie's cousins and their children and dogs. It was a lovely surprise and so exciting! At one point there were six of us doggies charging around by the river and having a great time.

After the fun at Water-Meetings, Julie and I went our separate ways from the rest of her family and for the remainder of the walk it was just the two of us. Julie called it "having some girly time" as the boys (Murdo and Digger) were back at home. We followed the path along through the fields and crossed the road at Roughlee where a large sign told us that it was "Pendle Witch Country." I wasn't sure what a witch was. I had heard that they were supposed to be scary, but looking at all the signs along the way, I thought they looked like fun!

We crossed the main road at Blacko and we could see Blacko Tower in the distance. We then continued through more fields passing an alpaca farm and up onto Weets Hill which stands above Barnoldswick. When Julie was young she had always been a little bit scared of Weets. Her grandma had once told her that strange lights had been spotted above the hill and the locals thought it was U.F.O activity. Grandma had once woken in the night and felt a strange urge to look out of the window towards the hill. She witnessed the strange lights herself, though she believed that U.F.O's were more to do with the government testing new aircraft than aliens. Today, as we crossed over the top of the hill and down into Barnoldswick, it was far from scary. The views were amazing for both Julie (who took photos) and myself (who stood on the top looking down to the animals on the farms below) and we thoroughly enjoyed it.

As we reached Barnoldswick, we walked down a lane in the direction of the town and we met an elderly lady walking her rather chunky Jack Russell named Terry.

This meeting was very traumatic for me. Terry was very friendly! Too friendly if you catch my drift! At first, as we approached, he acted all submissive and all seemed to be OK. However as we passed and my back was turned to him, he seized the opportunity to take me by surprise and jump on my back! Now as you can imagine, I don't take too kindly to being pounced on by strangers so I told him to back off in no uncertain terms. Luckily the lady who owned him was on my side and told me that I did right to have a go at Terry. I was in so much of a flap as we walked away that I fell off the pavement twice! We then crossed a busy main road and continued down past a school to the Leeds and Liverpool Canal. This took us along the tow-path for a couple of miles towards Thornton-in-Craven. We stopped at an outdoor café at Greenberfield Locks and I managed to wrap my lead around the plastic table leg, taking the table with me as we left.

At Thornton-in-Craven we should have passed through a farm but it is now a busy visitor attraction and there seemed to be a quad biking event on. The noise alone was enough to scare me. The path appeared to go right through the centre of all the commotion, so we did a slight detour and kept to the road. It was along there that we passed a gentleman visiting his female friend at her bungalow. They were saying their goodbyes as we reached them and they were both very keen to say hello to me and my human and ask where we had been. While Julie told them both about our walking challenges, I received lots of cuddles from the man. I got very excited about this and forgot my manners, jumping up onto his clean beige trousers with my muddy paws. Oops!

We walked 15 miles in total, ending the day in Earby. Julie's feet were very sore as new blisters had formed on top of the old ones from The Calderdale Way. We had such a good day though that she didn't really care!

Day 2, by Digger

Today we continued along The Pendle Way, walking 10.52 miles. However a lot of that was walked before we reached the Pendle Way. Our male human was working until mid afternoon and so could not help with the outward journey transport. We really wanted to carry on the walk but had no way of getting to the start point. We decided to walk there. It wasn't the best day on the walk as it was pouring with rain and we must have walked over 6 miles before we even arrived at The Pendle Way.

Julie decided to take both of us and soon regretted it. We were extremely wet and muddy and quite badly behaved. Mollie was dragging Julie around so much in the slippery mud that Julie fell over. The clumsy human landed on me as she fell. I screamed and Julie ended up with a jolted back. By the time we reached our continuation point at Earby, Julie was very stressed and we were really in bother. I had followed Mollie's bad example and become very giddy.

Julie had arranged for us all to be collected from a pub at Black Lane Ends, which is on the top road over the moors, heading back in the direction of home. There wasn't much for us to see on the route from Earby to the pub. We just plodded on through boggy fields. There was an amusing sign though on the gate of one of the fields. It showed a photo of a horse and it read; "Hello my name is Eric and I'm a fell pony and until recently I lived on the Cumbrian fells. I am 3 years old and I love people and will come to say hello. I won't harm you, I am simply inquisitive and want to be your friend. Please do not feed me. If I am annoying you simply raise your hand and tell me "No" or alternatively ignore me and simply follow the footpath. Please do not leave the gates open. Eric" We were quite keen to be Eric's friend too but sadly he was nowhere to be seen.

On greeting us at the end, male human cried "look at the state of you all!" as we were incredibly muddy. Back home he hosed us all down in the yard and I mean us all! Julie included! We were not impressed.

Day 3, by Digger and Mollie

On our third day of The Pendle Way, we had guests with us. Julie's aunt Soo, uncle Frederick, cousin Elize and their friend Vicky had all come up to visit us from Devon. They even brought their curly white fluff ball called Snookie. we had saved this part of the walk for them as they had wanted to climb Pendle Hill with us.

The route was not very long but the hill was steep. We ascended on the right hand side which has lots of uneven steps up it. This pretty much ruined Julie. Us Sprollies showed Snookie how it was done and we all had a great time. At the summit we bagged a trig point. It then began to snow a little bit and everyone loved it! On the way back down the slope was very gravelly. We were fine but Julie said it was a bit hairy. Or maybe she was talking about us dogs.... together with Snookie we had quite a bit of hair!

Day 4 by Digger and Mollie

We completed the next stretch of The Pendle Way the wrong way round for transport reasons. We started at Coldwell Inn and walked back to Black Lane Ends.

It was a beautiful sunny day and there were lots of people out and about. Two miles into the walk we met an elderly gentleman who stopped to chat. He told us that he volunteers for a wildlife agency and each day he climbs Boulsworth Hill (Which we were passing to our right) completing a survey on the birds that he sees. We looked over to Boulsworth and noticed that it was quite a long steep walk. The gentleman must have been very fit walking up there so often. We were very impressed with him and he was impressed with us doggies too when our human told him that we were walking to help wildlife and dogs.

For the main part of the walk we were wallowing in lots of muddy puddles and Julie had to keep telling us to "keep walking" yet when we did she complained that we were walking too fast! We saw lots of lapwings and plenty of other dogs. We even saw one dog in a pram! We wondered what the pram was as we are not used to seeing them. Julie explained that it was for pushing human puppies around in as unlike us clever dogs, it takes humans a lot longer to learn how to walk. She said that it was unusual to see humans pushing dogs around in one.

We went to take a closer look, Julie was hoping that we may be able to get a cheeky photo of it for our blog. Our timing was all wrong though. On getting nearer to the humans and their dog, it became apparent that the humans were having an argument. The lady (pushing the pram) was shouting at the man (on crutches) to cross a very narrow bridge. She was shouting "Get across for goodness sake!" and he was yelling back "I can't because I can't get my crutches on the bridge! It's too narrow!" They were very annoyed with one another. It wasn't a good time to ask for a photo of the dog in the pram.

As we passed through the village of Wycoller we saw lots of sign posts with witches on and a ruin of Wycoller Hall which is said to be the inspiration for Ferndean Manor in Charlotte Bronte's Jane Eyre. As dogs we had no idea what this meant. Julie said it was a book that is very famous and has sold millions of copies worldwide. We thought we would have quite liked Charlotte. We have similar ambitions.

As we left Wycoller we saw an old house with a headless plastic human outside. It was wearing a trench coat and there was a guitar propped up at the side of it. It seemed they were for sale. We didn't buy them. Dogs have no need for trench coats or guitars. Julie thought it was funny. We just think that humans are funny.

Day 5, by Mollie

The final stretch of the Pendle Way was very hot, lots of fun and very eventful. Digger stayed at home due to his fear of travelling in the van. The humans couldn't persuade him to get in it. Like the first part of this walk, it was just Julie and me, having some girly time together.

We set off at 8.45am to park the van at the end of the walk, back in Barrowford. Julie's dad Tony was then collecting us in his car to take us back to Coldwell Inn so that we could complete the loop.

"It's 12 miles" Julie informed Tony "So we should be finished by 2pm." Tony argued that it was a lot further than 12 miles but Julie insisted she had worked it out correctly and it was definitely 12. Julie hadn't worked it out correctly. By the time we finished we had walked 18 miles and it was 5.15pm!

As Tony dropped us off, he was complaining that he had been feeling a bit unwell lately and that he was rather cold today. It was quite a warm day so we were a little bit puzzled by this, though we didn't think too much of it and began our walk. We crossed a very lumpy field. Julie said it looked like there were lots of camels laying in the grass. I ran over the bumps and managed to find a tree to wrap my lead around just to add to the fun. We were heading towards a group trees and as we passed them we saw a young deer. This time (unlike the Calderdale Way) I managed to stay quiet and not scare it away.

Out of the trees and leaving the fields we crossed a cobbled ford in the road and I tried to get into the centre of the water and have a good wallow. It was a narrow road and Julie just about managed to haul me towards the side as an Asda delivery van came hurtling past. Further up the road we entered more fields and then joined a farm track past an old chapel and down towards Walverden Reservoir.

After a mad dash up a hill full of cows, we reached another lane, crossing a main road and onto Nelson Golf Course. There were signs here warning humans to "Keep dogs on leads and beware of flying golf balls." Who knew that balls had wings? It sounded scary! We didn't hang around there for too long.

It was around this time that Julie received a phone call from her mum. We had been planning to meet Lynn and Tony for lunch at some point on our walk and then Lynn was hoping to walk with us for a while afterwards. We presumed that the phone call was to find out our whereabouts for planning purposes but we were wrong. Lynn was phoning to say that after Tony had dropped us off he was taken ill and had been having palpitations and hallucinating. Lynn had taken him to hospital. We were very worried but we couldn't really do much other than continue walking.

As we left the golf course we became unsure as to which of three paths to take. We met a man and his dog and he boasted that he had run the Pendle Way as part of an event and he had beaten the record at the time and still held it to this day. We were impressed. Considering he seemed to be a bit of an expert on The Way, Julie asked him which was the correct path to take. He replied "I don't know! It WAS 20 years ago!" Luckily I managed to show my human the way and I took her past lots of houses before crossing a main road, a canal and then rejoining some lovely wildflower filled fields. This was where another little terrier type dog tried to have his wicked way with me. He was very rude! Just like Terry the Jack Russell. I can't help being adorable but it isn't half annoying when I am on a charity mission!

After a lovely paddle in the river, we came out onto a road where we had to cross an old stone bridge called "New In Pendle Bridge." While pondering the name, which was carved into the stone, the brake on my extendable lead came undone and I made a bid for freedom. I was so excited that my lead was extending that I didn't notice I had run out into the road. Julie screamed at me to get in, just as a car horn began to beep at us! I panicked and ran back to my human on the pavement but the horn carried on. I hid, human hid, (well she put her head down) and we waited for the angry motorist to pass by. It turned out not to be someone about to tell us off but Tony and Lynn on

their way back from the hospital! What a co-incidence!

As Lynn drove by, Tony phoned us to say he was feeling a bit better and after crossing the motorway bridge, following another beautiful river and a long hot hike up through more fields, we met them at Higham for lunch. They brought my brother Toby and we sat outside The Four Alls Inn in the sunshine. Toby was laid out on a posh rug that had been in Tony's car and the locals all thought it was funny to see a dog laid on a rug outside the pub. I wasn't so posh. I just made do with the tarmac instead.

It was while we ate, in Pendle Witch territory, that Lynn confessed to being a witch and casting a spell on Tony. She had poisoned him with something called Slippery Elm. Oops sorry, Julie is telling me off for not quite telling the correct story here. The correct version is that Lynn had tried to help Tony when he first became ill by giving him a herbal remedy from her cauldron (oops sorry, there I go again) I mean from the herbalist. When he was taken ill today they were panicking that the herbal remedy had poisoned him. It turned out that he had a kidney infection and that they can sometimes do scary things to you.

After lunch the path led us towards Lynn and Tony's home, so Lynn and Toby the dog came with us while Tony drove back for a rest. As we neared their home, Lynn and Toby went to check on Tony and swap Toby for my other brother Jack. We had great fun with Lynn. She goes down hills on her bum and she introduced us to a talking pig called Spot.

We arrived at a village called Newchurch where there is a church which has a mysterious "Eye of God" carved into the stone tower and one of the real Pendle Witches is said to be buried just outside the graveyard.

Crossing the road, we climbed a steep hill and then descended through some spooky woods down towards a reservoir at Barley. There we met up with Tony and Lynn again for an ice cream. I was treated to a little lick of Julie's ice cream and Jack was very naughty and pinched the whole of Tony's ice cream right out of his hand. Tony didn't mind though as he was feeling a bit cold again. We said that they should go home instead of Lynn walking to the end with us as planned and as they got into their car, I jumped in with them. Sod it, I thought! Julie can walk the last bit alone, I need a snooze! Julie dragged me out of the car but I just nipped around the other side and got back in again. I wanted to go back to Lynn's with my doggie brothers.

I was eventually persuaded to complete the walk, and after a further three miles we finally reached Barrowford and the welcoming sight of the van in the car park. We were shattered but very happy!

The Pennine Bridleway – Settle Loop

In May 2016 we completed the Settle Loop of The Pennine Bridleway. The bridleway as a whole, stretches from Derbyshire to Cumbria, almost parallel to The Pennine Way. There are two "Loops" in addition to the bridleway and we chose to walk the 10 mile loop above Settle in the Yorkshire Dales as part of our challenge. This was the shortest walk out of our 6 "Ways" and we completed in one day.

We also had a guest with us on this walk. A lady called Sue Stephens. She had previously completed a sponsored run in aid of our rescues, raising £130.

We woke Julie at 5.30 am even though her alarm was set for 7am. We were keen to meet Sue. Male human let us play outside for a while so that Julie didn't have to get up straight away and we wandered off into the field and ate a lovely breakfast of sheep poo. When we were let back indoors, Julie was still in bed so we jumped on her and breathed our poo breath in her face. Julie told us that we were disgusting and that we didn't deserve a walk. We still got to go though. We are the Furry Fund-raisers. She can't do it without us! As soon as Julie got up and began to get ready, we sneaked off back to bed. We needed to conserve our energy for the walk you see... and sleep off our breakfast.

The route led us out of the town square and up a road lined with cottages, then branched off a up a steep hill. We had only just set off and Julie was huffing and puffing her way up the hill. Sue is a keen runner so quite a bit fitter than Julie. She was very nice though and waited for Julie to catch up.

Once we were up on the hillside, there were great views both down over the town and across the dales to the Yorkshire three peaks. The sun shone all the way and for a change we were very well behaved. As we reached the moors leaving Settle behind us, the scenery became a bit less interesting but there were lots of smells for us Sprollies to investigate. The humans were too busy chatting to be disappointed with the great expanses of grass. As the route began to loop back around, there were views over Malham Tarn to our left. We were far more interested in the Highland cows which were grazing on the moorland. The cows were very interested in us too and they chased us. We all had to run away, fast!

The path which led us back into Settle was quite rocky and downhill all the way. As we neared Settle once again, we had some lovely views down over a different part of the town. We walked along winding lanes and passed the shops as we made our way back through the town. However all us dogs were interested in were the treats at the end. We had a quick stop off at the pub for drinks and dog treats. Mollie got a little bit too close to Sue, forgetting all about the rules of personal space and sitting herself on Sue's knee. Sue didn't mind one bit though. It was only a problem when Mollie decided that she would rather get on the table.

The Yorkshire Three Peaks

This walk was suggested to our humans by their friend Bryan, who had wanted to complete the walk himself and thought that it would be a great one to do as part of our challenge. It is a challenge to be done in a day, or 12 hours if you want to bag a certificate. It is a circular route taking in the mountains of Whernside (736 m or 2,415 ft) Ingleborough (723 m or 2372 ft) and Pen-y-ghent (694 m or 2,277 ft). Depending on where you set out from, it is roughly 25 miles in total.

We pencilled it in for the last weekend in May. After finding The Calderdale Way so difficult, Julie was quite nervous about this challenge. Three mountains in one walk is quite tough when you are rubbish at climbing up hills. What made it even more worrying for Julie was the fact that in the days leading up to the walk, it had been snowing! She had visions of either the walk having to be called off, or having to get the air ambulance out to rescue her from the snowy peaks. Neither of which she wanted.

Right up to the last minute, the humans were undecided as to which of us dogs to take. They worried that walking both of us may be a bit much for them as we do get a bit excited at times. We can be a bit of a safety risk on steep hills. In the end, male human didn't want either of us to miss out and reasoned that even though we are double trouble together, there would be three humans to help share the leads.

With rucksacks packed for all eventualities, the alarm was set for 4.30am. We reached the car park at Horton In Ribblesdale at 6.20am. Digger was so excited that he slipped the lead and ran into the road and Mollie pooped all over the car park. After a quick capture and clean up operation, we were all set to go. We logged our start time and set off up a country lane towards Pen-y-ghent.

It was a dry, sunny morning but quite cold. Perfect for walking as it prevented us from getting too hot on the strenuous parts. We didn't really understand how long the walk was going to be, despite the humans repeating to us that it was going to be a LONG ONE and that we should calm down. We had used a huge amount of energy just being giddy dogs, before we even reached the first peak.

The route up to Pen-y-ghent was quite short. It was gradual at first and became steep and rocky nearer the summit. There were lots of people climbing it and we were quite surprised as it was still very early in the morning. The higher up we climbed, the icier the rocks became and it became a little more difficult to get us all up there safely. In some places the humans were on their hands and knees. Obviously following our example, as we know full well that four legs are better than two. There was a covering of snow on the ground as we climbed and we wagged our tails as we checked out the views.

We reached the trig pillar at the summit quite quickly and were pleased to have ticked one mountain off the list so soon in the day. As we descended down the opposite side of the hill, we found it covered in much deeper snow. It was great fun and we were like skiing doggies all the way down.

The next part of the walk follows part of the Pennine Way and was the long stretch that led to Whernside. It was easy walking and the route was an obvious path. We then walked on the road for a while. It was flat but quite a distance. We tried to hurry along a bit because there was a fell race due to start back at Pen-y-ghent and we didn't want to get caught up in it.

There were lots of other people walking the Three Peaks, including a large group of Sikhs who take part in the walk every year in aid of charity. They were all really lovely and helpful and lots of them stopped and commented on how impressed they were that us dogs were attempting the challenge. It seemed that not many people took their dogs up there due to the height and distance. Our humans told them all about our "Walk for Wildlife and Woofers" challenge. They were all very impressed.

Before attempting Whernside, the highest of the three mountains, we stopped for lunch by a river close to the very impressive Ribblehead Viaduct. It was so cold that we didn't stay there for long. By the time we set off again there were walkers everywhere! The fell runners were also starting to catch up. Luckily the race took a different route up the steepest side of Whernside. Our route took us up a very long gradual climb. It was still hard going though. The climb never seemed to end and there were literally hundreds of walkers heading the same way. We were pretty much queuing all the way up the hill. We would stop for a breather and people would overtake us, then the same people would stop for a rest and we would overtake them. Our humans chatted to lots of them along the way.

As we neared the summit the snow became compacted and icy due to the amount of footfall. Then black clouds came rolling towards us bringing with them a hail storm. Julie fell down four times on this section. There were always lots of walkers to help her back up (Murdo and Bryan were further ahead) but on the fourth time she hurt her thigh and was worried she may not be able to carry on. Julie gritted her teeth and pushed herself up to the summit where we joined the path of the fell runners and things got BUSY! The runners didn't stop, they just carried on racing down the other side. We joined the walkers in the queue to get a photo at the trig pillar.

After a quick rest and some pain killers for Julie, we began our descent. It was chaos. We were caught right up in the race and where there wasn't ice, there was slippery mud. There were people falling down everywhere. It was like a game of human dominoes. We had to be very well behaved doggies and stay close to our humans. Julie cheated a bit at one point. The path was so slippery that she couldn't stand up so she found a section of thick snow, parked her backside on it and slid down the hill on her bum. She said it was like sledging but without the sledge. Luckily she managed not to hit any rocks. That could have been quite painful despite her ample bottom padding.

We had a break at the bottom of Whernside and then set off to the killer that was Ingleborough. This was the steepest of the three and like the top of Pen-y-ghent it was very icy on the rocks. Julie fell twice this time and the path was so narrow and crowded that if someone stopped (usually Julie) it caused gridlock behind them. Our humans were struggling and so were we, though Bryan was still doing well. We agreed to let him go ahead and we would meet him back at the car park. It was unfair for us to hold him back as he wanted to see how quickly he could complete the walk.

We reached the top of Ingleborough but then realised that it was not actually the summit. We were on top but at the lowest side. The trig pillar was at the opposite end. By the time we reached the pillar, Julie was so relieved she had to fight the urge to burst into tears. Once again we had to queue for a photograph and then we began our final descent.

As we made our way down the hill, Digger was off the lead and pottering about between the other walkers. Some of which were a Sikh family. Their two teenage girls were admiring Digger. One of them said to the elders that Digger reminded her of one of the spirits from their religion. Julie's ears pricked up because she finds these things fascinating. The girl asked one of her male family members if he thought that this particular spirit could be inside Digger. Digger was most alarmed! He hoped not, though the humans say that sometimes he can act like a dog possessed. The girl was informed that Digger would not have been possessed as the spirit she mentioned could not enter the body of a living being. It was just a free spirit. Julie loved this. It was one of the highlights of the walk.

As we completed the descent and headed back into Horton In Ribblesdale, we bumped into some walkers who we had passed a few times along the way. They congratulated us all on finishing the walk and were surprised that us dogs had managed it. We were a little bit miffed that they had doubted us. We were always going to manage it. It was the humans who struggled. Some of the Sikhs whom we had met earlier in the walk, invited us into a camp they had set up in the field. They offered coffee and toast for the humans and water for us. We would have loved to have joined them but we were attempting to complete the walk in the 12 hour deadline and we were getting very close to running out of time. In hindsight we should have accepted their offer because after rushing to the finish line to log our time, we missed the deadline by two minutes! Bryan managed it in 11 hours 2 minutes and we came in exactly an hour later at 12 hours 2 minutes.

The Dales Way

The Dales Way is an 84 mile (135km) walk stretching from Ilkley in West Yorkshire, up to Bowness on Windermere in Cumbria. It passes through the Yorkshire Dales, hence the name, and out of the 6 walks we had planned, this was probably the one we were looking forward to the most. We began on the 13th June 2016 but due to us having to match available weekends with available transport it took us three months to finish. We reached our destination on the 16th October.

Day 1 by Mollie

We began the Dales Way in typical Julie style, on the spur of the moment! On 13th June, midday, Julie said to me "I fancy starting it now! If we shorten the route we could begin this afternoon. Shall we?" Well you know me when it comes to walking for wildlife and woofers. I don't need to be asked twice! Male human said he would give us a lift to Ilkley and collect us later on from Bolton Abbey so we were set to go!

Due to the fact that we were looking forward to this walk, we were very giddy after being dropped off at Ilkley. We rushed along the riverside path to find the dry stone bench with the plaque which reads "For those who walk the Dales Way." This indicates the beginning of the walk and there is a matching one at the end. I posed on the bench very nicely and Julie was very proud of me as she took a photograph.

We left Ilkley through flat fields and alongside a river passing quaint old cottages and a caravan park. We then headed in to the village of Addingham. Everything looked very pretty in Addingham as the streets and houses were strewn with bunting. Julie told me that it was to celebrate The Queen's 90th Birthday! I quite liked it and wondered if I might get some when it's my birthday. In the meantime I settled for having my photograph taken in front of it all.

Leaving Addingham we headed through more fields towards Bolton Abbey where there is a ruin of an old priory. Julie thought it was beautiful and wanted to go inside and have a look. I was more interested in getting down to the river. Inside the priory walls it suddenly became rather cold despite it being a warm and sunny day. Julie's imagination ran away with her again like it does. She thought that it may be haunted and that ghosts were flying through it.

We approached the bridge and the stepping stones which both crossed the river. On arrival there was a bit of a commotion. Despite the signs warning of a fast moving current and of the water being deeper than you think, a young couple were trying to get their dog to cross the slippery stepping stones. The girl was on the opposite side of the river and the boy on our side. The dog was halfway across, clinging to a stone after having fallen in. It was very distressed. Both humans were shouting at the dog to come to them and the poor thing was confused and crying. Some other humans were telling the dog owners off for being irresponsible. It was horrible to watch. Luckily the dog eventually made it across but it was very upsetting to witness. We took the safe route and went over the bridge. From there we walked further along the opposite side of the river to the Cavendish Pavilion Cafe which was to be the finishing point for that day.

There is a field along the way which has been left for nature to take over as an experiment. The grass is high and there are lots of wildflowers. Among them lay a large log which frightened the life out of me as we passed. I did a double-take and literally fell over myself in the process. Julie thought it was funny but she made sure that I was ok by giving me a big cuddle and then treated me to a lick of her ice cream as we waited for our lift at the end.

Day two, by Digger and Mollie

We continued on the Dales Way on the 19th June and we also hit our 300th mile for this year. We set off from the pavilion where Julie and Mollie finished last time and we walked to the village of Burnsall.

Our walk took us into Strid Wood and past a "Bodger" in his hut. We had never heard of a bodger before. It turned out that he is a craftsman who makes wooden items using traditional methods. Julie bought a hand carved "Lucky Elf" on a string. It was supposed to bring us good luck on our walks. She named him Dale Sway, a play on Dales Way and also fitting because he sways on his string as we walk.

This part of the walk was quite busy with other walkers and dogs, though they all seemed to be local day visitors. We couldn't find anyone else who was completing The Dales Way.

As we continued further into the woods we came across The Strid. This is a narrow looking stream that runs through the rocks and as innocent as it looks it has apparently killed everyone who has ever tried to jump it. Due to the wide river suddenly having to fit through the narrow rocks it causes the water to gain speed and depth. There are deep chasms below into which the undercurrent drags anyone who falls in. The problem is it doesn't look dangerous from above. It gives the impression that you can just stride across, hence the name "The Strid." We had to look at this death trap from quite a distance as Julie didn't trust us to get anywhere near it.

Following the river along, we then crossed it passing the village of Appletreewick and onwards towards Burnsall. It was around here that Mollie had a little accident. The lucky elf didn't bring her much luck. As we walked along a narrow path, Mollie decided she was thirsty and tried to take a short-cut down the grassy bank to the river. Hidden in the grass though, was a bees nest. Poor Mollie stuck her head right in it and then leapt straight back, yelping. Bees covered her face, stinging her all over. It was very scary. Mollie was distressed and looked like she was having a fit. Julie tried to help her but she was wriggling around so much that it was impossible. Then, almost as if it had never happened, Mollie returned to "Adventure mode" and went off down the path full steam ahead. Julie muttered "Where there's no sense there's no feeling" and the incident was forgotten about.

On arriving at Burnsall we had a rest on a bench overlooking the river. Julie checked Mollie's face. There were a few lumps and bumps but she was fine. After a quick snack we made our way back to the start. We even met a squirrel and a woodpecker on route.

We stopped at a pebbled beach by the river, just as we clocked our 300th mile. Julie took a photo of us to mark it. There were lots of crab claws among the pebbles and we had a good old sniff at them as we don't usually see crab claws. Julie thought they were only found at the seaside. Male human later told us that you can get fresh water crabs in rivers. We will have to be careful in future. We don't want to get our paws nipped! By the end of the walk we had covered 14 miles. We had a wonderful time.

Day 3, by Mollie

The third stage of our Dales Way walk fell on the 14th of July which just happened to be my 7th birthday! Julie chose me to do this walk with her for that reason.
We packed our bags early morning and headed off to a village called Buckden. This was our destination for the day. We had our lift, Tom, following us in his car so that we could leave the van at Buckden and he could take us back to the start point at Burnsall. I travelled in the car with Tom as Julie talks too much when she is driving and I was too tired from the early start to listen!

The walk took us through more fields and along the river once more until we reached Linton Falls (Where a bridge crosses the waterfalls) and from there we took the right pawed turning up towards the town of Grassington. We walked up the high street to the top and from there down a narrow lane, leading to a grassy path across the moors. This bit was wonderful! It was so pretty with all the wildflowers in the grass and there were lots and lots of birds. The path was easy to follow so we could just wander along and enjoy the views. There was an old lime kiln along the way and I had a good sniff around inside it. We then reached "Conistone Pie" which turned out not to be a pie at all! Talk about gutted! Instead, it was a big rock on the hill that apparently looked like a pie.... But it wasn't a pie.... There was no big juicy meaty tasty pie.

We stayed at the "Pie" for 15 minutes. I'm sure Julie

was just rubbing it in! She recorded a short film on her phone there and took some photos of me posing with my birthday card. It was a very hot day and there was no natural water anywhere for me. I had already drunk all mine and most of Julie's bottled water.

We carried on along the grassy path and past some bracken which I ran into and tangled my lead round just as a group of walkers approached us. Julie was scrabbling around in the bracken trying to untangle me as they arrived. She gets embarrassed when I misbehave. Especially if the oncoming folk have a nice well behaved dog which this group did. It turned out that these walkers were also tackling the Dales Way but were walking it from top to bottom. They asked Julie how far Grassington was and warned us that Dent Dale was very boggy. Fantastic! I just love bogs!

Onward we walked, through the woods and down a bridleway towards the road. We followed the road for a short while before entering a field to our right. After that it was like an assault course. Stile, field, stile, field, stile all the way to Kettlewell. I felt like an olympic hurdler! By the last field I was exhausted and very hot and thirsty. Luckily there was a metal trough full of water for the sheep. I sneaked a bit of it, hoping that the sheep wouldn't mind. Rehydrated, we continued on our way into Kettlewell village. Kettlewell was great! There were steps down by the bridge to the river. We rushed down them and while Julie sat on the steps I lay in the river for a whole ten minutes. Heaven!

We then visited The Cottage tea rooms where we got a table outside and ordered lunch. The lovely lady there asked Julie if I might like a free sausage. Seriously!! Free sausage!! I was frantically trying to communicate "YES!" Luckily Julie knows me well and told the lady that I would really enjoy a sausage. Especially as it was my birthday. Oh it was wonderful I tell you. It nearly made me forget the stone pie. Well almost....

Due to the lack of water on the first leg of the journey, Julie stocked up at the café. If she had looked at the map though, she would have realised that the rest of the trip was alongside the river and I didn't need any.

The second half of the trip was nicer for me as I spent a lot of it in the river paddling. However Julie found it a little dull compared to the first half. It was very similar all the way along the path. Arriving at Buckden the van was waiting for us but we enjoyed some time sitting on the grass before making our way home.

Day 4 by Digger

On the 8th August we continued on the Dales Way. As we left home it was cold, wet and windy. In fact it had been windy all night and Julie had lain awake worrying about being stuck up Cam Houses (The Dales Way's highest point) in bad weather. We needn't have worried though, because in Buckden the sun was shining.

Our male human was supposed to be on a training course but as Tom drove Julie and I out of the yard, he came running down saying it had been cancelled. He decided to come with us which was great news as today's walk was quite remote in places. Tom dropped us all off at Buckden and went off on his own adventure, while waiting to collect us all later.

We walked along a lovely stretch of river through Hubberholme to Yokenthwaite where we passed a stone circle. Then the path led us through Deepdale, Beckermonds and Oughtershaw. It was very pretty and easy going as it was flat. I just happily plodded along and didn't even need to be on my lead. At Oughtershaw there were a few things to look at, a stone carving surrounded by baby goats for example. The humans became so distracted taking photographs that they missed the turning and climbed a mile or more up the road before noticing. We could see the correct path parallel to us down below us. There was only a rush filled field between us and the correct path. Or a two mile detour via the road. We decided to go into "Stealth

Mode" sneaking down through a gully in the field and over a wall at the bottom. It was great fun and I was so excited about scrambling down through the field that I kept forgetting that we were supposed to be hiding.

The path from here was a little monotonous. It took us up a long drag of a hill to Cam Houses which is one of Yorkshire's wildest and most remote farms. From here the humans pointed out Ingleborough in the distance and said that it was hard to imagine that we climbed it back in May alongside Pen-y-ghent and Whernside. Today we struggled just to get to Cam Houses. Once at the summit we saw a stone cairn and the sign post showing that the Dales Way meets both the Pennine Bridleway and the Pennine Way. It was very cold and windy up there, even though the day had turned out to be fine and sunny. We could see why the guide book advises to avoid this section in bad weather.

The descent was easy, down a long gravelled road where we met lots of other walkers and some cyclists too. When the road ended we had reached Gearstones where Tom was waiting for us. We had walked over 15 miles and were all a bit tired. When we arrived home, Julie went to get in the shower and her back gave in. I spent the evening snoozing on the sofa and Julie spent the evening squealing in pain.

Day 5, by Mollie

29th August was a Bank Holiday Monday which meant that the humans didn't have to work. On top of that we were offered some transport so we got to walk our next stretch of The Dales Way. Hooray!

We set off from Gearstones and we walked over some very boggy moorland towards Dent Head. I absolutely LOVED this part as I got to run free and there were lots and lots of muddy puddles! I had the time of my life up there, though the humans weren't too keen on the muddy bits and they preferred the views instead.

At Dent Head there was a big viaduct and we stopped for photos and a train passed over. We really enjoyed this part of the walk. From Dent Head we walked through Cowgill where we went off track slightly to look at another viaduct called Arten Gill. A lot of the walk today was along the road and was a bit sore on our feet. However there were some nice riverside stretches too.

We walked through a campsite just outside Cowgill and Julie was wondering why a family were pitching their tent on the path. She said to Murdo "They have all the field to choose from and pitch their tent right on the path!" Then, as we passed them, Julie managed to embarrass herself. She had to bypass the tent blockage and walk on the slippery muddy slope which resulted in her falling and being sat in the mud in front of the campers! Oops!

That wasn't the first time today that Julie embarrassed herself.... We had to walk through a plantation at Little Town and she inhaled a bug and then tried to choke to death on it! Male human and I didn't stop to help. We pretended we didn't know her and ran off!

The path into Dent was the most narrow path we have ever walked on. It was literally one paw behind the other just to fit on it! Julie fell over about five times as she is so clumsy! She said there wasn't room on the path for her big boots, though Murdo managed easily with his even bigger boots.

Arriving at Dent we found a mounted Dales Way map by the path and checked our progress. We have come a long way but the remainder (despite it only being two more sections) looked like such a long way still!

Leaving Dent was just as difficult as entering it! The stiles were so narrow we struggled to fit through. As you cross the road there's one at either side and they are literally only leg width. I managed to squeeze through at a push but the humans had to pull themselves up and right over the top of the walls to get their bums over!

From Dent we continued through fields and along narrow roads over to Millthrop which was a very

pretty village. A lady had made a doggie water station outside her house. There was a model of a dog made from old wellington boots and a bowl to drink from. I loved it and so did the humans.

After a brief spell off the route after getting distracted by the wellington boot dog (It was right on the junction where we should have turned and we went ahead instead) we headed towards Sedbergh where we saw an old tower-like building called the Pepper-pot. It was a lottery funded refurbishment and it was quite interesting to see but we couldn't go inside.

At Sedbergh we met Tom who was waiting at the crematorium to pick us up or bury us, depending on what state we were in! We were in a bit of a state to be honest, all sore and limping a bit, but we weren't so bad that we needed a headstone! Phew! We walked just over 16 miles and it was great fun!

Day 6 by Mollie

On 15th October I was the "Chosen One" to go on the next section of The Dales Way from Sedbergh to Grayrigg. Well, I was actually backup after Digger refused to get in the car again! He had a major tantrum and wouldn't go. I tell you, I didn't need to be asked twice! I was straight in there!

Tom gave us a lift and we set off on a really interesting part of the walk. We had wished that our male human

was with us as there were lots of things he would have liked to see on this section. We passed old railway bridges and viaducts and an old post office that had been converted into a house.

We were really loving The Dales Way (even though it was taking us an eternity to complete) and Julie and Murdo were already thinking of doing it again even though we'd not finished it yet.

At Lowgill I got Julie down on her bum as I dragged her down an embankment to the river Lune! She is putting "Pants with a padded bum" on her Christmas list! (Though male human said her bum doesn't need any more padding. It has enough!) We walked over ten miles on this section and went home to dream happy memories from today's walk.

Day 7 by Mollie and Digger

WE DID IT!!! On 19th October 2016 we finally completed The Dales Way! 84 miles from Ilkley to Bowness on Windermere. (Though we actually walked further as some parts we walked twice... and on occasions got a bit lost)

It was a lovely sunny day, just perfect for finishing this amazing walk. We set off bright and early while it was still dark as the start of today's walk was a long drive away. By the time we arrived at Grayrigg it was daylight but the moon was still in the sky.

We were both so giddy that we dragged the humans along for the whole 16 miles! Mollie pulled harder than ever and managed to snap her lead and Digger tried to follow her at such a pace that Julie had rope burns on her fingers!

The first 3/4 of the walk was lacking in scenery so most of our photos were taken towards the end. However we met two lovely ladies called Donna and Liz who were also walking (and finishing) the Dales Way today. The humans had great fun chatting to them as they were the first Dales Way walkers that we had met who were going in the same direction.

As we approached Windermere the scenery suddenly improved and the humans took photos of the dramatic mountains in the distance. We Sprollies couldn't wait to get to the big lake at the end.

When we reached the end of the Dales Way we found the bench which matched the one at Ilkley. We went to get our certificates from Hawkshead Outdoor Shop. Digger was so exhausted that he collapsed in the shop and fell asleep! The humans then took us to a lovely pub that not only let doggies in but gave us treats too. Tom was waiting for us there to bring us home. We ate and drank and had a lovely snooze by the fire. After a well deserved rest we then nipped down to the lake as it is customary for Dales Way walkers to dip their paws in the water! It was fantastic! What doggie dreams are made of!

Lady Anne's Way

Lady Anne's Way was the final walk of our "6 Ways in 2016." At 100 miles, it was also the longest. We had such a good time walking it, we would say that it was probably the best!

Lady Anne Clifford was born at Skipton Castle in 1590 and died at Brougham Castle in 1676. After inheriting the family estate in her fifties, she spent the rest of her life travelling between her castles and renovating them. This walk is based on some of the routes she had taken while visiting the many buildings on her estate. It begins at Skipton Castle in North Yorkshire and ends at Brougham Castle in Penrith.

Day, 1 by Digger

17th October 2016. RAAARGH! My name is Digger and I'm big and I'm tough and I am mean! I am NOT scared of the van and Julie did not have to drag me off the bed, out of the house and across the yard to get me into it this morning! Honest! I was very brave and travelled in the front with Julie all the way to Skipton (a massive 4 miles away) and that was where we began our 6th challenge "Lady Anne's Way."

We parked in a big car park and walked up through the busy town to Skipton Castle. As people set off in their suits to work, we set off in our walking gear to Penrith!

We left the town and had to cross a very busy bypass, and we then had to negotiate a golf course. As we mentioned earlier in the book, we are not too keen on crossing golf courses. As we approached it, Julie told me that the instructions said to follow the very clearly way marked path of green posts. On our arrival we saw a line of green posts running right through the centre of the course. So of course (no pun intended) we followed them. Until we got shouted at that is. All the golfers started a commotion and because they were all trying to tell us things from different directions, we didn't understand. "Go to the green posts!" They shouted, and pointed to the right where there was one solitary white post. Confused, we ran across to it and found on closer inspection that it was a very very pale, almost white, shade of green. We wondered if the golfers had been colour blind. It wasn't our idea of green.

After that things were pretty much straight forward and we crossed fields towards Embsay. We passed an old house, outside which was a hedgehog driving a car. I had to go and check if it was OK as it didn't appear to be moving. I kissed it and Julie laughed and said it was an ornament. I was so embarrassed as she somehow managed to get a photograph of me kissing it. We travelled through Eastby and along Bark Lane. Was this an instruction for me to bark, or something to do with tree bark? Human words confuse me. I decided that it was probably tree bark so I stayed silent.

Further on we arrived at a children's play area and Ice Cream Parlour which caused no end of confusion for human Julie, as it appeared to have been built on the path! The map showed the path to go straight through the play area. We saw a post where a way mark had obviously been removed and when we asked, we we're told there was no footpath there. After 15 minutes of wasting time wandering round the car park searching for the path, we ended up having to walk to the road to make a detour.

The rest of the walk was quite easy and in addition to Bark Lane earlier, we passed through Dog Kennel Plantation, though it was nothing interesting and there were certainly no dog kennels to be seen. We continued slightly uphill and then descended down the moor towards the road that lead to our destination for the day, the ruin of Barden Tower. Once on the road we walked down to the tower which Julie took lots of photos of. She loved it. I couldn't understand what all the fuss was about. There were no dogs, rabbits, or even other humans. There was nothing there to excite me!

We had planned to catch a bus back to the car park at Skipton but there were none due for quite some time. Instead we had to wait an hour for male human to come and pick us up. I didn't mind though, I was in no rush to get back and Julie gave me lots of treats as we waited.

Day 2 By Mollie

29th October. Today was foggy, boggy, soggy and a little bit Halloween scary too! The whole walk was a bit of a battle. The first issue I had was trying to get Julie out of bed. She didn't want to get up which was most unusual. She finally managed to drag herself out of bed just 20 minutes before our lift arrived. We left home at 8am and it was very misty and drizzly. We were continuing along Lady Anne's Way and ending the journey at Buckden. Tom followed us there so we could leave the van and then drove us back to where we needed to start.

The first few miles of the walk were pretty miserable weather wise and by the time we got onto the moors above Grassington we couldn't even see where we were going for the fog! This stretch of the walk follows the line of the Dales Way to Kettlewell but further up the hill. We did the Dales Way section on my 7th birthday in July and that stretch was one of our favourites for the views and the weather. Today however was the total opposite. The guide book promised "extensive views" but with the thick fog I could only just see my paws!

We followed the paths (which were quite wide and clear so that was a bonus) and crossed over moors where there were ancient settlements and also disused mine shafts. A couple of miles in we passed an abandoned farm house called "Bare House." It was open and deserted. There was no road leading to it, it just sat there all lonely on the moors. Julie approached it to take a photograph but suddenly got a case of the heebie jeebies! She said it was like something out of a scary movie all eerie and enveloped in fog. As we passed through the gate beside the house, we checked the guide book and saw that it advised us to take an alternative route down the hill into Conistone if the fog was bad. Julie was undecided what to do. It was VERY foggy but she wanted to walk the proper route rather than the escape route. Especially as there was a trig pillar further ahead. We decided to be brave and take the true path. We turned right, crossing the back of the house towards a wall corner. We weren't brave for long though. We suddenly heard a loud "Wooooooooaaaaaaahhhhhhhh" from the deserted house. We were both pretty scared to say the least! Luckily there wasn't a ghost but there was a young calf and it was charging at us! We ran away thinking that if we could just get round the wall corner, it wouldn't be able to see us any more and it might stop. We hadn't considered the fact that there might be a whole load more cows around the corner. We ran right into the centre of them. They were all incredibly nosey and as they began to approach us we panicked and ran as fast as we could away from them.

Due to the fact that we were sprinting through the fog, unable to able to see where we were going, we ended up totally off track. After a short detour we arrived back on the path and climbed safely over the wall, on top of which I tried to shake all the mud off my coat and onto the guide book.

After passing through more fields, we were accosted by more cows and were getting pretty worried. We couldn't go on but we couldn't turn back either. We waited a while and then decided to run for it again.

Once more we ran in the wrong direction and this time into an area of disused mine shafts! The guide book said "Stick to the path" as it was a dangerous area. There were warning signs all over the fields and on the gates. There we were in the middle of the "danger zone" and in thick fog! We eventually joined a bridleway and things became a little easier. By the time we reached Kettlewell (about 2 hours later than planned) the fog was lifting but it was now pouring with rain. We stopped for lunch in the same café that we went to on my birthday while walking the Dales Way. This time I was not offered a sausage so Julie shared her sandwich with me instead.

From there we followed the path to Buckden via Starbotton and again it was literally parallel to The Dales Way, just on the other side of the road.

When we finally reached Buckden, a group of cyclists rode past us and they all shouted hello to me.

"Good afternoon doggie" they said. "Hello pooch!" They must have known that I am a bit famous now. I'm like a doggie superstar! What's that Julie? Big headed? What do you mean?

I got Julie to drive me home after that so I could relax my paws... It had been a long day.

Day 3, by Digger

13th November. Today we reached our 600th mile this year! Continuing on Lady Anne's Way and setting off from Buckden. It was very scenic at the start and we met lots of other doggies. We then climbed up onto the moors and things began to get a little bit bleak. We also began to get a little bit lost. There were lots of tracks up there you see and where the guide book said "follow the obvious track," the track that was obvious to Julie wasn't the one that the writer was talking about! Reaching a hill called Addleborough, Julie became totally confused with her map reading and kept heading towards the hill instead of passing it. We must have approached it from three different angles before Julie realised we should have been passing it instead. It got to the point where we were probably not walking Lady Anne's Way at all. It's hard to imagine her running around the moors in all directions like we did! We were so relieved when we finally came to a road again!

As we passed through the village of Worton we realised that we would be reaching our 600th mile somewhere near Nappa Hall. The hall was not owned by Lady Anne but she stayed there on the way to her properties. It is said that Mary Queen of Scots had stayed there for two nights and also that James I had visited. Julie was very pleased that we would reach 600 miles there and was imagining taking photos of the beautiful building. However when we arrived it was a bit of a let down.

The magnificent front face of the hall was facing the opposite direction to where we were on the path and it was also hidden by trees! We took a photo of the back door (that was as good as it got) and then it began to rain. It was not really the celebration we had hoped for. Still, that was one of our two challenges completed. By the end of the day we had beaten last year's mileage.

Day 4, by Mollie

14th November was a funny day. Julie hadn't been sleeping well for the past week and on top of that she woken up with toothache. She was stressed about finishing the walk and it was also raining and cold. Male human had accidentally locked her walking boots in his shed and gone to work, so there was a drama about finding the shed keys. It wasn't going to plan. We finally set off only to be told that the road that we needed to go down was closed due to flooding. Our detour got us stuck behind a very large and slow moving tractor for miles. Nothing seemed to be going our way.

We had a discussion in the van (or rather Julie did. I just listened and yawned) about whether fate tries warn you against things by making everything go wrong, or if you make your own fate by being determined to overcome the obstacles. It was all a bit weird for me... I think the lack of sleep was getting to Julie. Anyway we decided that only time would tell and we would wait to see the outcome of the day. As it turned out, there was no reason for fate to warn us off this walk and our determination to get there through floods and rain rewarded us with a fantastic day! Arriving at the start of our walk the sun came out and a rainbow appeared. It stayed fine for the whole day and we walked through woods, past waterfalls, through quaint little hamlets and ended up at the lovely town of Hawes.

Day 5 by Mollie

15th November. OH WHAT A DAY!!!! We had one of the BEST WALKS EVER! The sun was shining, we were continuing Lady Anne's Way and everything about the day was just perfect!

We set off from Hawes in the morning to head towards Pendragon Castle, a ruin that was supposedly built by Uther Pendragon, father of the legendary King Arthur. We passed through the village of Appersett and saw lots of farm dogs in their kennels by the side of the road. I wanted to go over for a sniff and to say hello but they were making such a fuss that we decided to move on before the farmer came out.

We continued down the road passing Rigg House, a home which was once owned by some of Julie's ancestors. Julie was very interested to see the house, as when she was researching her family tree she found out an interesting story about it. It was once believed to be haunted but only in one room in the centre of the house. The owners at the time simply demolished the centre of the house to get rid of the ghost and now it stands as two separate buildings.

Further along, we left the road, crossed a stile and climbed a big steep hill. Julie struggled but I dragged her right up there! At the top there was an old lime kiln and the views went on for miles and miles. Just like the rabbits! I loved the rabbits!

As we reached the top it levelled out onto an ancient highway and we followed it all across the hillside towards Outhgill. I was ultra excited today and ran around like I was an Olympic athlete on performance enhancing drugs. Julie bobbed along behind me on the lead screaming. She just can't keep up.

We passed some old ruins of an ancient inn and a house called High Hall. Julie loved these old buildings and tried to imagine the olden days when the inn had visitors arriving on horse and cart, glad of a drink and a break in their journey. She told me that in those days it had probably been a busy road, yet now it was so isolated it was hard to imagine there being an inn up there. We crossed a bridge called Hell Gill which went over a very deep and narrow ravine. I had to be kept on the lead at this point. There is a local legend that a highwayman leapt over this ravine on horseback to escape capture. Julie likes all these old tales so she was very excited about the places we had seen. I was more interested in all those furry rabbits bobbing around!

At one point, the air force must have heard that we were around and treated us to a fly over like they do with the Royal Family. We had jets and Apache Longbow helicopters flying right over us! What's that Julie? Not a flyover? A training exercise? Rubbish! They were all for me! I just know it!

Further along we came across a sculpture called "The Water Cut" standing proud on the hillside. I had my

photo taken in the centre of it. Someone pointed it out later, that it looks like a giant coffee bean, but then being a dog, I've never seen a coffee bean so I wouldn't know! After the sculpture we began our descent from the hillside. Arriving at the village of Outhgill, we visited a small church which Lady Anne restored. We went to find the carved stone plaque above the door which was put there to commemorate the restoration.

This church was also the resting place for a lot of workers who sadly died while building the Settle to Carlisle railway and were buried in unmarked graves.

As we continued the walk we spotted our destination. Pendragon Castle. Julie went a little bit funny. It was just a pile of rocks to me but Julie thought it was all a bit special! She was very giddy about it, the way that I get when I see a rabbit. However I was more excited to see Tom waiting there to take us home. I do enjoy our car rides home.

Day 6, by Mollie

On the 27th November we walked 11 miles from Pendragon Castle to Brough Castle (It should have been less but we went the wrong way and back at one point.) I went instead of Digger because he was being soft again about travelling. It was a lovely sunny day but quite cold. It rained a little at the start but we got over it. Once more there was lots to see.

At the beginning there was a rainbow shining down onto Lammerside Castle ruins. It looked amazing and Julie told me all about the saying about a pot of gold where the rainbow ends. There may have been a pot of gold under the castle but we didn't stop to look. We were on an important mission you know!

At Kirkby Stephen we crossed the Coast to Coast path! I saw the sign and got very excited when Julie informed me that it was a 192 mile walk. Julie just looked at me and said "You have got to be kidding Mollie! 192 miles? Seriously?"

Further along we heard a commotion in the trees and Julie stopped still, puzzled. Two big red birds flew over us and Julie said "PARROTS?" and guess what? She wasn't hallucinating! There were lots of red, green and blue parrots in the trees in front of an old house! It turned out that the house was called Eden Lodge and was once owned by a nature and animal lover who rescued feral parrots. The birds still live there and we are guessing this man's family

must do too because there were lots more birds in big aviarys around the back. There was also a pet graveyard at the bottom of the garden, with headstones listing the names of the owners beloved animals.

We came to a village called Winton where there were red squirrels EVERYWHERE! Julie has only ever seen one in her life and today we saw dozens! It was very exciting! I loved watching them running up the trees! I became an expert squirrel watcher in minutes. I spotted them a mile off. It was so exciting!

When male human phoned Julie to see how she was doing, he was worried that she had eaten some dodgy mushrooms from a field. "Parrots and red squirrels?" he asked "are you sure that you are not seeing things?"

The next stage took us through boggy fields and over a busy road to Church Brough and there we visited the very impressive Brough Castle. This was the largest of the castles we had seen so far. Tom was waiting to give us a lift home but we all walked up to the castle first to have a good nosey. Julie was very impressed! I was more interested in the ponies that were there in the grounds. They were very tame and they let me sniff them and say hello.

I slept all the way home while Julie and Tom planned the rest of the walk. We were almost at the end.

Day 8, by Mollie

4th December. Today we walked our penultimate stretch of Lady Anne's Way! Only one more walk to go and we have completed both this "Way" and our yearly challenge of walking "6 Ways in 2016" Once again Julie didn't sleep last night (the excitement gets to her!) so when she packed her bag at 6am she forgot a few things... Like her map, her guide book and her money! Nothing too important though... She remembered me thank goodness!

I wasn't supposed to be on this walk as I have done the last 2 sections but we are having major issues getting Digger to come if he thinks he has to go in a vehicle to get there. After 5 mins of faffing around trying to get me to stay and Digger to get out of bed (even trying to pull him out by the lead) Julie relented and let me go and Digger stay.

Tom drove us back to Brough Castle where I woke up the whole neighbourhood by getting a little bit over excited! My barking echoed throughout the small square where we had parked. It was then, as we arrived at the Castle, that Julie realised she had forgotten the map and guide book. She laughed because the night before, her dad had asked her if she takes a compass and she replied "No because I can't figure out how to use it!" He was telling her off and saying that she needed to learn to use, and carry a compass. We wondered what he would say to her walking without a map too!

After setting off we encountered our first problem. A river without a bridge. I was fine and splashed around in the water but Julie was slipping on the stones trying to cross it and ended up with soaking wet feet! "Half a mile into a 15 mile walk and my feet are already cold and wet!" she cried. Then I snapped my lead and legged it! To which Julie yelled "*****! *****!"

We think we stuck to the majority of the official route but in some places we went a bit off track. It wasn't an overly interesting stretch of the walk. Lots of plain fields and not much to see. When we arrived at Appleby the Castle was closed. We were very disappointed. That is the half of the point of this walk, to see the castles! It was closed as it was out of season for tourists but it was so warm and sunny it was hard to remember that it was December. Julie tried to stand in the Castle gateway and get a photo from a distance but failed miserably. She was blocking the driveway and ended up almost having a heart attack when a car crept up behind her and blew its horn. Its occupants, an elderly couple, were in hysterics because Julie jumped so high she almost flew out of her walking boots!

Tom met us at Appleby and looked after me while Julie went into the church to see the graves of Lady Anne and Lady Anne's mother. We then left Tom and continued for another 4 miles to Long Marton. We were adding a bit on now in order to try and shorten

the final stage. We just managed to sit down outside the church at Long Marton, when Tom arrived and we were so stiff and sore that we struggled to get back up again. Once home we planned our final walk. Julie said that just thinking about it made her want to cry with relief that we had almost finished at last!

We'd had the best time ever completing our walking challenges but for most of the year all Julie had done was work and walk. She was looking forward to having a teeny bit of free time in order to do other things. Like sit still for an hour or two. Boring!

Day 7, by Digger

11th December 2016. WE DID IT!!!!!!! We finished our 6th and final Way and our challenge for 2016!

Julie set the alarm for 5.30 am (despite the fact that yet again she didn't sleep and pretty much kept the rest of us awake too!) and we drove with Tom to the starting point of our walk. We were all a bit tired and grumpy at that point.

On arrival at Long Marton (where we ended the last stage) the humans went to get us out of the car and Julie said "Murdo! Mollie isn't well. She is having a fit!"

The humans had to lift Mollie down onto the grass and look after her while they waited for it to wear off. It took some time and we were all worried about whether Mollie would be able to complete the walk or not. She has had fits before, so the humans were used to it but it had been a while since the last one.

Five minutes later Mollie was back on her feet and trying to drag Murdo across the road. We decided that we would set off and see how she was. Tom said he could find us and collect her if she was too poorly and we could meet her at the end. Tom didn't need to collect her though, she was her usual self throughout the walk "Steam train in full pulling power mode."

The first three quarters of the walk were a little bit dull, both weather wise and walk wise. We had been told this by others who had done the walk. It is lacking in points of interest compared to the rest of the walk and a large section of it is along a narrow road with fast moving traffic.

We left Long Marton and walked towards Kirkby Thore, a small village with some pretty houses. Crossing the main road we walked along the river for a while but recent floods had dragged lots of litter up into the trees and it all looked a bit messy. At Ousenstand bridge we joined the road for a while, passing behind Crossrigg Hall where there were some interesting old buildings and a bridge over the river. The guide book said that one of the buildings was haunted and that there was an archway under which no dog will pass. We didn't get to investigate though, as it was all fenced off. When we got to Cliburn we walked along the scary road for couple of miles. We sat on some boulders by the animal sanctuary (which appears to have closed down) and ate lunch. Our legs were hurting at this point from all the road walking.

At Clifton Dykes we left the road but maybe should have stayed on it as the path was so boggy and the stile between the fields was surrounded by deep water. We had to cheat a little and do a quick, cheeky detour to avoid the flooded stile.

Further along we walked down a tree lined path and Mollie ran under the blackthorn bushes, wrapping her lead round the furthest one, not once but twice! Julie had to crawl under on her knees to unravel her. The thorns scratched her head and Murdo laughed and filmed her complaining, with her backside sticking out from the bush.

After this, things got a little more interesting as we arrived at Brougham Hall which had a huge fancy door knocker in the shape of a lion's head. The hall was being restored so there was a lot of scaffolding around. We didn't stay long. We were almost at the final castle. We dashed off down the road and there it was! Brougham Castle! Tom was there waiting to walk the final approach with us. We got to the entrance and realised that we had to pay to enter the castle and guess what? The humans had forgotten their money! "Oh no!" Julie cried! "Now what?"

Luckily for us, the lady in the castle's shop was really lovely and let us all in. Even though we dragged mud all over her nice carpet and Mollie knocked a toy off the display! The lady made a huge fuss of us and congratulated us on our walks. It turned out Tom and Murdo were both entitled to free entry anyway through membership cards that they have so it was just Julie that was sneaking in.

We were over the moon to have completed another year long challenge for our rescues and we managed to raise £2900. It was wonderful that we had been able to combine our hobbies with raising money for Wildlife and Woofers.

BROUGHAM CASTLE
6 Ways in 2016! DONE!!!!

Along the way..

Lots of exciting things happened to us along the way.... A lovely lady called Kelly Gaze designed us our own fabulous logo. We featured in full page articles in a magazine and a newspaper. Ordnance Survey used a photo of Digger's Paw on their Instagram page. We were Cover Dogs for Pendleside Hospice's Facebook page and we cared for some orphaned hedgehogs!

We have raised over £5000 to date and are currently in the middle of a new challenge for 2017 and planning another one for 2018.

Keep up to date with our adventures at www.facebook.com/500miles2015

Thank You!

We would like to thank our male human Murdo for all his support and for letting us go off walking so much. We woof you very much!

Lynn & Tony for their sweet selling skills, transport and company on the Pendle Way. Tom for transport on the Dales Way and Lady Anne's Way. Corinne for editing our book and lending us Lee to accompany us on the Calderdale Way, Lee for walking with us.

Thanks to Sue, for her fund-raising race and for walking The Pennine Bridleway with us.

Kim, Laura, Eva, Scarlett, Rose, Emma, Peter, Aileen Catherine, Calum , Bryan & the McShaws for joining us on some of the walks. Thanks to our cheerleader Sandra for motivating us along the way, to Stephanie Delooze for getting our story in the press and Stephanie Murie for assisting us with our four rescue hedgehogs. You have all been superstars, helping us on our fundraising journeys.

To all our sponsors and Facebook followers and all those who said "You should write a book!" This is for you! Thanks to all those who bought it. All proceeds are to be split between the rescues that we support.

Woofs from Digger and Mollie xx